The Skip

A play

Mary Rensten

Samuel French—London
New York-Toronto-Hollywood

© 1995 BY SAMUEL FRENCH LTD

Rights of Performance by Amateurs are controlled by Samuel French Ltd, 52 Fitzroy Street, London W1P 6JR, and they, or their authorized agents, issue licences to amateurs on payment of a fee. **It is an infringement of the Copyright to give any performance or public reading of the play before the fee has been paid and the licence issued.**

The Royalty Fee indicated below is subject to contract and subject to variation at the sole discretion of Samuel French Ltd.

> Basic fee for each and every
> performance by amateurs   Code D
> in the British Isles

The publication of this play does not imply that it is necessarily available for performance by amateurs or professionals, either in the British Isles or Overseas. Amateurs and professionals considering a production are strongly advised in their own interests to apply to the appropriate agents for consent before starting rehearsals or booking a theatre or hall.

LINCOLNSHIRE
COUNTY COUNCIL

822

ISBN 0 573 13304 2

Please see page iv for further copyright information

CHARACTERS

Muriel A lady who likes everything to be correct, including her dress. One for appearances rather than feelings. Together with Olga she runs an antique shop. Late forties.

Jessie From Lancashire. She looks what she is — a "no-nonsense" bag-lady. She wears an old coat, boots, a woolly hat, and gloves with the fingers cut off. She may have had a good figure once, but now she's just a small, round ball. She has difficulty in walking. Dependent upon her friend and partner, Alice, of whom she's genuinely fond. Sixties.

Alice Tallish, in her youth she must have looked elegant. She has seen much better days, but she still has style and sparkle. She tops off her old, tattered clothes with an Ascot hat, bedecked with flowers, fruit, and two pheasant tail feathers pointing upwards. Late sixties, even seventies. It's hard to tell, and Alice wouldn't dream of telling you.

Olga English is not her first language. (She could be French, German or Scandinavian.) Muriel may have the class, but it's Olga who really knows about antiques. She normally wears a track suit, of which Muriel does not approve. In her early forties.

The Tramp We don't even know her name. In the hierarchy of "collectors" she is the lowest. She can't even stand upright. She probably smells horrible and only a swig from a bottle keeps her warm.

The action of the play takes place in a suburban street

Time — the present

COPYRIGHT INFORMATION
(See also page ii)

This play is fully protected under the Copyright Laws of the British Commonwealth of Nations, the United States of America and all countries of the Berne and Universal Copyright Conventions.

All rights, including Stage, Motion Picture, Radio, Television, Public Reading, and Translation into Foreign Languages, are strictly reserved.

No part of this publication may lawfully be reproduced in ANY form or by any means — photocopying, typescript, recording (including video-recording), manuscript, electronic, mechanical, or otherwise — or be transmitted or stored in a retrieval system, without prior permission.

Licences are issued subject to the understanding that it shall be made clear in all advertising matter that the audience will witness an amateur performance; that the names of the authors of the plays shall be included on all announcements and on all programmes; and that the integrity of the authors' work will be preserved.

The Royalty Fee is subject to contract and subject to variation at the sole discretion of Samuel French Ltd.

In Theatres or Halls seating Four Hundred or more the fee will be subject to negotiation.

In Territories Overseas the fee quoted in this Acting Edition may not apply. A fee will be quoted on application to our local authorized agent, or if there is no such agent, on application to Samuel French Ltd, London.

VIDEO-RECORDING OF AMATEUR PRODUCTIONS

Please note that the copyright laws governing video-recording are extremely complex and that it should not be assumed that any play may be video-recorded for *whatever purpose* without first obtaining the permission of the appropriate agents. The fact that a play is published by Samuel French Ltd does not indicate that video rights are available or that Samuel French Ltd controls such rights.

THE SKIP

A suburban street

A back-drop, or back-projection, depicts the front doors and steps of terraced Victorian houses, in the process of being "gentrified". In front of the houses is a pavement with coal covers. On the road in front of one house is a mini-skip, with the legs of a chair poking out. There is litter— crisp bags, a beer can, etc. — in the gutter. Beside the skip are several full black polythene rubbish bags, two of them open at the top, with garbage spilling out

Muriel enters. She walks with a firm, determined stride, carrying before her, with disdain, a large, white chamber-pot decorated with red and yellow roses. She dumps, almost drops, it into the skip, brushes off her hands, makes a sound of satisfaction at a job well done, glances momentarily at the chair, then marches back the way she came

As Muriel nears the exit, she passes Jessie and Alice entering. They are both pushing battered shopping trolleys (bags on wheels). Alice is wearing an exotic hat (see character notes p.iii), at the sight of which Muriel lifts her eyebrows

Muriel exits with a wry smile

Alice halts, looks at the skip. Jessie walks on, realizes Alice has stopped and turns back to her

Jessie You'll not find owt there, Alice. You did that one yesterday.
Alice Indeed I did, but that, my dear Jessie, was yesterday. Who knows what treasures may have been secretly deposited during the hours of darkness?

Jessie Oh ay ... just the odd diamond necklace, old Ming vase ... Well, go on then, have a look. As tha says, who knows.

Alice No, no. I wouldn't want to waste your time, Jessie. I know how precious it is.

Jessie Oh, I've nowt pressing. Not for a while, any road. Queen's not expecting me at Palace till gone three.

Alice Oh, well, in that case, I think we've got time.

Jessie (*taking from her trolley a wooden box which she places upside-down beside the skip*) Go on, get on with it. Up you go.

Alice hitches up her coat, revealing thick, patched trousers, and steps on to the box, then from there into the skip. It's a well-practised routine

Alice (*reaching down*) Aha!

Jessie What you found? Summat good?

Alice Exceedingly good, Jessie. Exceedingly good.

Jessie Well, come on, then. Don't keep it all to yourself. Let's have a look.

Alice (*looking over*) Patience, my dear. Patience. (*She burrows down into the skip again*)

Jessie They'll not like it if I'm late, you know. They did say three.

Alice (*putting her head over the side*) Three?

Jessie At Palace!

Alice Oh, at the Palace. Yes, well, there are some people one mustn't keep waiting, of course. I'll be with you in just a moment. (*She disappears into the skip again, almost immediately throwing several pieces of tattered cloth into the air to land on the ground*)

Jessie (*looking at the rags in disgust*) Rags? Alice, we don't do rags.

Alice (*looking over the side of the skip*) Jessie, Jessie. The rags are for wrapping.

Jessie Wrapping? Oh, right. Wrapping what?

Alice (*flourishing Muriel's chamber-pot*) This, my dear Jessie. Ta-rah! (*She steps down from the skip*) Isn't it splendid?

Jessie I don't see owt splendid about that. It's a po.

Alice Oh, Jessie, you are common. A po! Dear, dear. This is an artefact of rare beauty.

The Skip

Jessie Get on with you. It's a po!

Alice Oh, Jessie. You just have no eye for the finer things of life.

Jessie Humph! Finer things of life ...

Alice Just look at these roses. They are exquisite. See ... little buds even. Can't you see how beautiful they are?

Jessie All right, all right, so it's got pretty flowers. It's still just a po.

Alice (*looking lovingly at the pot*) We had one just like this when I was a child.

Jessie Well, lucky you, we had an outside lavvy.

Alice There was a basin, and a jug ... And a soap dish. All matching. All with flowers. I can see them now — in the guest room. Yellow curtains, a white counterpane, a blue carpet with a border of yellow ...

Jessie Yes, well my mother was genteel and all. It was just me dad that wasn't. Now come on, is there owt else in there?

Alice (*coming out of her reverie*) Um?

Jessie I said, are you going to look for owt else? Or are you going to stand there all day reminiscing about your glorious past?

Alice (*handing down the pot to Jessie*) Here. Take it. And don't drop it. (*She climbs down, taking the pot from Jessie and starts to wrap it in the rags*) Right. Shall we depart?

Jessie Depart? With just that? You could at least have another look.

Alice My dear Jessie, for today this beautiful pot (*she pats it*) will suffice. (*She puts the pot in her trolley*)

Jessie (*putting the box back in her trolley*) You're barmy, d'you know that?

Alice It's a happy state, Jessie. Being barmy.

Jessie I don't know why I put up with you. I really don't. Not when you're like this.

Alice Jessie, Jessie ... Who else do you know who would make you a gift of a chamber-pot ornamented with roses?

Jessie I don't want it, you barm-pot. It's no use to me.

Alice Oh, very well. You scorn my gift, I shall leave. (*With her head held high, she begins to walk off*)

Jessie Alice.

Alice (*turning back*) Yes?

Jessie Come back here.

Alice Why?

Jessie Because you've forgotten your pusher, you dozy ha'p'orth.

Alice (*turning back*) Oh.

Jessie (*what shall I do with her?*) I don't know ... Is it summat you've been eating, or what? You're getting worse, you know. You've not been having a go at the spirits, have you?

Alice Jessie, Jessie. You know I wouldn't dabble in that. Never.

Jessie Eh? I'm talking about the spirits you drink, you stupid old bat. You've not been at the meths, have you?

Alice Jessie, Jessie, how could you think such a thing? Meths? Me?

Jessie Keeps out the cold.

Alice gives Jessie a "look"

So they say.

The Tramp shuffles on, carrying a bag. Mumbling to herself, she is bent over, never rising above waist level

Alice If I ever thought that you ... (*Pause*) Oh, Jessie, we're not reduced to that. Oh no. No.

The Tramp peers into the open rubbish bags, roots around and extracts a couple of food packets which she shakes before putting in her bag. Alice and Jessie watch her

Nor that.

The Tramp becomes aware of them and looks up

Tramp Bleeding skippies! Toffee-nosed lot. (*She spits and moves on, mumbling*) Think themselves above everybody else, they do. (*To her imaginary friend*) Well, we know different, don't we? (*She turns back to Alice and Jessie*) Up yours an' all. (*She lifts two fingers at Jessie and Alice; to her "friend"*) You don't want to take no notice of them. (*Shouting, to Alice and Jessie*) Skippies! Who'd you think you are? (*To her "friend"*) Come on, let's not

The Skip 5

stay here. I'm not having them watching me. (*She sticks out her tongue and blows a raspberry*)

The Tramp shuffles off, mumbling

Pause

Jessie I think I used to know her.
Alice Surely not?
Jessie She used to do the skips ... I'm sure it's her ... Till her leg got bad and she couldn't climb ... (*During the following she starts to cry*)
Alice Oh, Jessie ... My dear ... As long as my legs are strong you have nothing to fear. Years of riding, you know. (*She pats her thigh*) That's what it is. Riding.

Pause

(*Noticing Jessie crying*) Oh, for goodness' sake ... (*She picks up a spare rag*) Here! Blow your nose.
Jessie I'm not going to blow my nose on that, thank you very much!
Alice It's clean.
Jessie I'm still not blowing my nose on it. (*She pauses*) You wouldn't.
Alice I would.
Jessie Go on then.

Pause. Alice blows her nose on the rag

Alice There. Satisfied?
Jessie Ay. You'll do. Come on, shove that back int' skip, and let's get going.

Alice tosses the rag into the skip

What about yon chair? Did you look at it?
Alice Um?

Jessie The chair ... in the skip.
Alice Oh. No, it's broken. What I could see of it. I couldn't lift it out anyway, not on my own.
Jessie Oh, if only I could just get up there.
Alice Well, you can't, so stop worrying about it.

They start to move towards the exit, crossing the stage as if continuing their walk along the road

Jessie It's not just in me mind you know, it is in me legs.
Alice I've told you — as long as my legs are strong ...

And they've gone

Olga enters from the other side, carrying a kitchen stool. Olga is incensed, eyes flashing, lips pressed together. She stops at the skip, places the stool beside it, climbs up and is about to get into the skip when Muriel enters, following her with a mocking smile on her face

Olga How could you! You had absolutely no right, Muriel.
Muriel (*patronizing*) Oh, do stop it, Olga. You're being ridiculous. We agreed. We would not sell reproductions.

Olga starts burrowing into the skip

What are you doing?
Olga (*straightening up*) It's not there! It has gone!! (*Pause*) I don't believe you ever put it in there. You have broken it, haven't you?
Muriel Of course I haven't broken it! I told you, I put it in the skip.
Olga So where is it, then?
Muriel I don't know. Somebody must have taken it.

Olga looks unconvinced

Well, people do, don't they? They just come along, and take things out. For all I know those two women could have taken it.
Olga What women?

The Skip

Muriel Oh, just a couple of old women who were passing. Tramps, by the look of them

Olga sits dejectedly on her stool

I'm sorry.
Olga No, you are not. You are not one bit sorry.
Muriel Yes, I am. I didn't mean to upset you.
Olga Hm.
Muriel If you choose not to believe me that's up to you. (*Pause*) I'm not sorry I threw away the pot, I'll tell you that!
Olga What does it matter whether it was reproduction or whether it was old. It was a beautiful pot, and I liked it.
Muriel We said at the beginning, when we started up together, that we wouldn't sell repro. Only the genuine stuff. As soon as you let in one piece of repro, you're just opening the floodgates ...
Olga It was the way that you did it! You did not ask me, you did not discuss it. It was not yours to take, Muriel! It was mine. What if I had bought it as a present for someone?
Muriel Oh, Olga, no. You hadn't?
Olga I might have done! Why should I not?
Muriel Well ... it's up to you, of course, but I would never give something in such bad ... something like that.
Olga You think it is bad taste?
Muriel Yes, I do, frankly.
Olga But you would give as a present something that is damaged?
Muriel I would not!
Olga You would, if it was an antique.
Muriel Ah, well. That's different.
Olga (*laughing cynically*) If it is old and it is broken, it is OK; if it is new and you do not like the taste ——
Muriel What?
Olga Taste. You know ... (*carefully enunciating*) taste. Not to your taste. Yes?
Muriel Yes.
Olga If it is not to your taste, it is no good. It has something to do with being English, I think.

Muriel It has nothing to be with being English. Anyway, I'm not English!

Olga All right, then, British. The British Empire. The old order. Things must not change. I think that is why you so like all these Victorian things; they belong to a time when Britain was great, and in your mind you wish to believe it still is. Well, I have some news for you. The world has moved on, and repro has its place. If only because it is providing work for people to do. (*Pause*) As it happens, I did not want to give the pot away, I wanted it for myself.

Muriel Whatever for?

Olga Well, what do you think I wanted it for?

Muriel A repro chamber-pot? (*Pause*) I don't know. Plants? Pot-pourri? (*Pause*) Oh, no, not for ... Oh, Olga.

Olga Well done, Muriel. Yes, I wanted it for when your genuine, Mr Crapper original, Victorian water closet does not work!

Muriel It's only just occasionally that it doesn't work.

Olga Half the things in our house do not work. Oh, they look wonderful, oh yes, but you can take style too far, you know. Besides, it is like living all the time in the shop. I am surprised you have not put prices on everything! You really must not get so obsessed with this business of things being antique.

Muriel I am not obsessed, Olga. We had an agreement.

Olga Yes, I know we had an agreement. I just did not realize it applied to the house as well.

Muriel Not everything in the house is antique. We have electric light.

Olga So we do! (*Teasing*) Maybe one of these days we will get a washing machine.

Muriel Yes, of course. I have no objection to that.

Olga Oh, Muriel. (*Pause*) I do not see why we cannot have some repro stuff as well.

Muriel starts to protest

No, listen — not all repro is bad.

The Skip

Muriel pulls a face

And I can think of some repro that you would like very much to have.

Muriel Oh yes?

Olga For instance: if someone were to offer you a piece of sculpture, a Michaelangelo copy of a Greek statue, would you turn it down on the grounds that it wasn't genuine?

Muriel Oh, don't be stupid!

Olga It is what he did. Well, answer my question.

There is no response from Muriel

Come on, Muriel, admit it, you would take it like a shot.

Muriel Well ... if I was sure it was genuine.

Olga (*laughing*) Oh ... genuine what? Greek?

Muriel Oh, this is pointless. You know very well that's not the same thing.

Olga (*laughing*) It is.

Muriel I'm not having repro in my shop.

Olga Our shop.

Muriel All right, our shop. Have your pot in the house if you must, but ——

Olga Yes, well, that is all a bit academic now, seeing it has gone. The trouble with you, Muriel, is that although you are a very good businesswoman, you just do not think about people's feelings!

Muriel I've said I'm sorry. I don't see what else I can do about it. (*Pause*) All right, I'll buy you another one.

Olga is not listening. She is looking at the chair in the skip

Well, you could say thank you.

Olga (*looking up, softly*) Muriel.

Muriel (*miffed*) What?

Olga This chair ...

Pause

Muriel Well, what about it?

Olga It's Regency.

Muriel (*as if the sun has suddenly warmed her*) No?

Olga Look for yourself. I may not have a taste in chamber-pots, but if I say that a chair is Regency ...

Muriel (*climbing on to the stool and looking into the skip, then turning round to Olga*) Oh, Olga. It is. Oh, it's beautiful. Oh, how could I have missed it? Oh, help me to get it out. (*She tugs at the chair, then sees someone offstage*) Oh, Lord, there's someone coming.

Olga So?

Muriel (*scrambling down from the skip*) I'm not going to be seen taking something out of a skip!

Olga Oh, *mon Dieu!* I just do not understand you. You will dig about in a rubbish tip for hours and hours, yet you will not be seen taking a chair from a ——

Muriel It's illegal to take from a skip.

Olga Who says it is illegal?

Alice enters with her trolley

Muriel (*whispering*) I'll come back for it later.

Muriel exits

Olga (*calling after Muriel*) Muriel! Where are you going? I cannot take it out by myself! (*Shaking her head*) She is mad, that woman. Crazy.

Alice That — madam — is ours.

Olga Pardon?

Alice That skip. It's ours.

Olga The skip. It is yours? Oh, I am sorry, I did not know. (*She moves the stool quickly*) We were not ... I was not taking anything, I was just ...

Alice They are all ours.

Olga All? (*Puzzled*) I do not understand. You mean you are the owner? It is your company?

The Skip

Alice (*laughing*) Now that is indeed a glorious thought. To own a skip.

Olga Well, if you are not the owner, what do you mean?

Alice We work them, my dear, we work them.

Olga You work them? Oh, you mean scavenging.

Alice (*hurt*) Well ... that's hardly the way I would phrase it, but——

Olga You mean you take out the things and sell them?

Alice Provided they are saleable. There are times, of course, when it's all rubbish.

Olga But sometimes you will find something that is really worthwhile, yes?

Alice (*wary*) Sometimes.

Pause

Olga You ... um ... you wouldn't by any chance have found a — a chamber-pot, would you?

Alice A chamber-pot? Why, have you lost one?

Olga Well, not exactly lost. (*Bitter*) My friend threw, well, no, she did not throw ... I hope she did not throw ... she says that she put one in this skip.

Alice Oh.

Olga It was white, and it had red and yellow roses painted on it.

Alice And it was of some value, I take it?

Olga Of course it was.

Alice In what way?

Olga (*surprised to be questioned*) In what way? Well ... in the way that beautiful things are valuable.

Alice Ah, I see. Not its monetary value, you mean?

Olga That as well. (*Getting riled*) Chamber-pots are collectors' items these days.

Alice (*couldn't sound more surprised*) Really?

Olga Yes, really. Genuine ones, that it.

Alice Genuine ones?

Olga Ones that were made to be used. Victorian ones.

Alice Ah.

Olga And ones from the Twenties ...

Alice Oh, from the Twenties as well. That is interesting. Mmm ... what would you expect to pay for, say, a Victorian one?

Olga Well, that would depend upon where you bought it, and the condition it was in.

Alice Yes, I see. (*Pause*) Let's say ... well, one in good condition, from an antique shop. Like that one down the road, for instance.

Olga Oh, well — fifty pounds. Sixty perhaps. It would depend.

Alice As much as that? My word ... they've certainly appreciated in value since the days when I used to use one.

Olga laughs

We did, you know. Cold passages. Unreliable plumbing.

Olga Oh, I know. I know about English plumbing.

Alice Just supposing I were to — to come across your ... chamber-pot. One never knows. It's surprising what one does find. What would you be prepared to pay for it?

Olga Oh, I don't know. (*Pause*) Fifteen pounds?

Alice stares Olga out

Twenty?

Alice Twenty. Is that your best offer?

Olga For fifteen pounds, I could buy a new one.

Alice I'm sure you could but we're not talking about a new one, are we?

Pause

Olga It is not a question of whether or not it is old. It is a valuable pot and I would like very much to have it back. (*Pause*) Twenty-five pounds, then. And that is my last ——

Alice Done! (*She shakes Olga's hand, opens her shopping trolley and takes out the chamber-pot wrapped in rags*)

Olga Oh! That is my pot! You mean — all this time you had it in your ... ? You took it out of the skip and now you are trying to sell it back to me? Oh, no, that is not right. What you are doing is criminal!

Alice It is not in the least bit criminal. (*Pause*) The question is — do you want it?

Olga Well, of course I want it! (*Pause*) There is something very strange going on here. If you had not met me, here, at the skip, what were you going to do with that pot?

Alice I would have put it back.

Olga In the skip?

Alice Yes.

Olga But why?

Alice Ah, well, you see ... my friend, Jessie, we're business partners ... well, she didn't like the pot. She didn't want it in the ... in our ... in the place where we both live. She doesn't have my eye for artistic things, you see.

Olga I thought you took the things so that you could sell them?

Alice No, no. Oh no, not always. There are occasions when we use the things we find. If they are of use to use, that is. But, if we are not going to sell them, and we have no use for them ourselves, then we return them. We have a code of practice. It's all very ethical.

Olga You are telling me that if I had been here just five minutes later, my pot would have been back in the skip and I could have taken it away?

Alice Yes.

Olga So, if in five minutes I could have taken it, I am not now paying you twenty pounds for ——

Alice Twenty-five.

Olga I am certainly not paying you twenty-five.

Pause

Alice We could come to an arrangement.

Olga Arrangement? What sort of ... arrangement? I am not doing any deal with you about something that belonged to me in the first place.

Alice Help me with the chair and you may have the pot. For nothing.

Pause

Olga The chair?
Alice (*smiling*) Much more in Jessie's line. She's a very practical soul, Jessie.

Pause

Olga (*looking at the chair*) That ... chair?
Alice Yes. I can't move it on my own. I would be most obliged.

Olga looks at the chair, then at Alice, and back to the chair

Olga No, I'm sorry. That would not be fair.
Alice Why not?
Olga Well ... a chamber-pot for a Re ... for an old chair.
Alice Very well. Then I'll take the pot away. (*She begins to pack the pot away in her trolley*) You're quite sure? You don't want it?
Olga Not on those terms, no.
Alice Right. Well, I'll be off. Good-morning.

Alice begins to move off, slowly. Olga looks again at the chair and a wicked look comes on to her face

Olga (*thinking "It would serve Muriel right"*) No, wait.

Alice turns back

OK. I agree. (*Almost to herself*) I shall live to regret this, I think.
Alice I'm sorry, I didn't hear what you said.
Olga Oh, it was nothing. Come on, let us take down the chair.

Alice puts down her trolley, starts to clamber up beside Olga

Give me your hand, I will help you up.
Alice It's all right, I can manage. (*And she gets up on to the skip*)

The Skip

Together they pull at the chair. Ad lib dialogue to be worked out according to how the chair is taken down, etc.

Oh please, do be careful, that leg's almost off ...

Olga I am being careful. Whoever put this in here did not intend it to come out ... A little bit more on your side, I think.

Alice heaves the chair up. It's been harder than she thought. She pauses, gets her breath

Alice (*expelling her breath*) Oohh ...
Olga Are you all right?
Alice (*still a bit out of breath*) Yes. Yes. Just a bit — puffed, you know.
Olga (*looking down into the skip*) It is fascinating to see the things that other people throw away. Look, there is a toaster. And an old radio ... Oh, and a teddy bear. (*She lifts a teddy bear out of the skip*) Oh, that is sad. (*She strokes its battered face, then gently puts it back in the skip*) Oh, and look — a typewriter! You would think they would get that repaired.
Alice "How shiny once, and beautiful."
Olga Um?
Alice "Fresh and newly born." Now they're all unwanted. Run down and worn out. (*Pause*) It's what happens when you're old.

The Tramp shuffles on, bent over as before, muttering to herself. She ferrets in the bin bags. She doesn't see Olga and Alice

Olga It does not always happen. There are some things that increase in value as they become older.
Alice Like chamber-pots, you mean?
Olga Yes. And chairs.
Alice (*observing the Tramp*) Pitiful. The depths to which some people sink. To spend your life rooting around in other people's rubbish. Very, very sad. Very sad.
Tramp (*seeing Olga and Alice*) Skippies! Bleeding skippies. Who you think you are? (*Chanting*) "I'm the king of the castle, get

down you dirty rascal." (*She sticks out her tongue, shakes her head, wiggles the fingers of one hand by her head, in a rude gesture, then moves on*)

The Tramp exits

Olga and Alice watch her

Olga (*appreciating the irony*) Yes, indeed. Very sad. (*Turning back to Alice*) Are you all right now?
Alice What d'you mean? (*Bridling*) Am I all right?
Olga Just now you were out of breath.
Alice Oh, yes. Yes, I ... Thank you. Yes, I'm quite all right now.

Together they pull at the chair and it comes free

Olga Be careful now. If you get down I will hand you the chair.

Alice gets off the skip. Olga hands her down the chair, then gets down herself

Alice (*inspecting the chair*) Hm ... Very nice. Very nice indeed. (*Looking up at Olga*) Get a new seat and some polish on it. Hm, yes. Yes, I think Jessie will be very pleased with this.
Olga Now that you have your chair, perhaps I could have my pot?
Alice Ah, yes, your pot. (*She gets it out and hands it to Olga. Looking at the chair*) I think it's genuine.
Olga (*looking at the pot*) Do you?
Alice (*still looking at the chair*) My grandfather had a set of these. I remember as children we used to put them all together in a line and crawl under them. He used to get so cross. My goodness, when I think what they would fetch now ... (*She looks up*) Um? Oh, not the pot. No, no, the pot's reproduction. Should you want another one, by the way, you'll find them in the market. Eight-fifty apiece. (*She puts the chair on her trolley*)
Olga Eight-fifty?
Alice Yes, that's right. Eight-fifty. With flowers. The stall is just

round the corner from that new antique shop. (*Pause*) Well ... it's been a pleasure doing business with you. Good-morning. (*She trundles towards the exit with the trolley*)

Olga is left standing holding her pot

Muriel enters, nodding to the passing Alice

Muriel (*seeing the chair*) Oh, no.

Alice, and the chair, go off

Muriel draws herself up to her full height. If looks can kill, Olga hasn't long to live. Slowly Muriel walks towards Olga

Olga ...
Olga Muriel ...

Pause

Muriel holds out her hand for the pot. Olga takes a deep breath and holds it out to her with both hands, like a sacrifice

Curtain *or Black-out*

FURNITURE AND PROPERTY LIST

On stage: Mini-skip. *In it*: chair, rags, battered teddy bear
　　　　　　Crisp bags
　　　　　　Beer can
　　　　　　Rubbish bags (full). *In one*: food packets

Off stage: Chamber-pot (**Muriel**)
　　　　　　Battered shopping trolleys (**Jessie** and **Alice**). *In* **Jessie**'s
　　　　　　　trolley: wooden box
　　　　　　Kitchen stool (**Olga**)

LIGHTING PLOT

Practical fittings required: nil
One exterior. The same scene throughout

To open: General exterior lighting

No cues

EFFECTS PLOT

No cues